Barreling Over Niagara Falls

By Nancy Kelly Allen

Illustrated by
Lisa Fields

PELICAN PUBLISHING COMPANY
GRETNA 2013

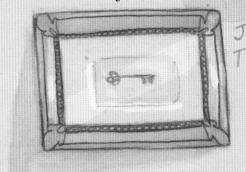

The word "Pelican" and the depiction of a pelican are trademarks of Pelican Publishing Company, Inc., and are registered in the U.S. Patent and Trademark Office.

Library of Congress Cataloging-in-Publication Data

Allen, Nancy Kelly, 1949-
  Barreling over Niagara Falls / by Nancy Kelly Allen ; illustrated by Lisa Fields.
    p. cm.
  ISBN 978-1-4556-1766-1 (hardcover : alk. paper) — ISBN 978-1-4556-1767-8 (e-book) 1. Niagara Falls (N.Y. and Ont.)—Juvenile literature. 2. Taylor, Annie Edson, 1838-1921—Juvenile literature. 3. Women daredevils—United States—Biography—Juvenile literature. I. Fields, Lisa ill. II. Title.
  F127.N8A45 2013
  971.33'903092--dc23
  [B]
                                                    2012029021

Printed in Malaysia
Published by Pelican Publishing Company, Inc.
1000 Burmaster Street, Gretna, Louisiana 70053

Annie Edson Taylor dreamed big. She always had.

When she played the piano, she dreamed of being a music teacher—and was.

When she danced around the house in Auburn, New York, with her three sisters, she dreamed of owning a dance studio—and did.

But when Annie played tag with her four brothers, she never dreamed of becoming a famous daredevil in the rough-and-tumble world of stunts—not once.

When the sizzle fizzled out of teaching music, and the fizzle sizzled out of teaching dance, sixty-two-year-old Annie had no job and little money. Tingling fear nagged her with every breath, every minute, and every day as she faced the grimmest future of all: the poorhouse.

A few days later, Annie read in a newspaper that Buffalo, New York, would host the Pan-American Exposition of 1901. The Exposition attracted thousands of tourists, who would be sure to travel to nearby Niagara Falls. A new dream of fame and fortune burst wide open and whipped Annie's fear of the poorhouse into courage.

Annie would do what no one had ever done—ride over Niagara Falls in a barrel. A vision played out in her mind of people traveling from far and near to meet the daringest daredevil of all, Annie Edson Taylor. People would buy her autographs, pay to have pictures taken with her, and purchase tickets to hear her story as she traveled around the country meeting and greeting fans.

Annie followed in the business footsteps of William Leonard Hunt, known as the Great Farini. Hunt tight-rope-walked over Niagara Falls and later traveled the world telling his story and selling trinkets. In Annie's dream, fortune followed fame.

Annie tucked away barely enough money for food and rent and spent the remainder of her savings to make her dream come true. She hired the West Bay City Cooperage Company to build the barrel that she designed to fit her body and keep her safe. Annie explained how she would perform the stunt and walk away unharmed. The barrel maker thought Annie's idea was big all right—big and foolish.

Annie's big idea created a big list of problems. How would she keep the barrel upright during the float down the river? How could she cushion the barrel so she would live through the dangerous ride?

Annie worked day and night to solve the problems. While most people feared for Annie's life, Annie pushed the fear of debt and homelessness to the back of her mind while she held on tight to her dream.

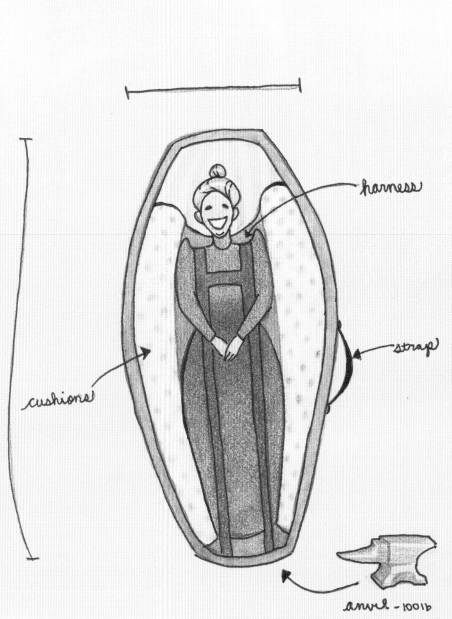

harness

strap

cushions

anvil – 100 lb

Annie placed a one-hundred-pound blacksmith anvil in the bottom of the barrel to keep it floating upright. She lined the barrel with a mattress and pillows to cushion the fall over Niagara. She also used a harness to hold her snug inside the barrel. Rescuers needed a way to hook the barrel and pull it out of the water at the foot of the Falls, so Annie had straps attached to the outside.

As soon as Annie solved one problem, another popped up. Annie needed a watertight barrel to keep from drowning. When the barrel maker oiled the oak to make it watertight, the barrel became airtight. How could Annie breathe in an airtight barrel?

Annie dreamed up another big idea. She asked the barrel maker to drill a hole in the side of the barrel and pump air inside with a bicycle pump. The barrel maker would plug the hole with a cork just before she began her stunt.

Annie hired a promoter, Frank M. Russell, to advertise her daring feat. Mr. Russell splashed ads in newspapers far and wide with news of the amazing, have-to-see-it-to-believe-it barrel ride over Niagara Falls.

One newspaper reporter asked Annie if she thought she would survive the fall.

"The barrel is good and strong and the inside will be cushioned so that the rolling movement will do me no harm," Annie answered.

The newspaper reporter wasn't convinced.

On October 24, 1901, Annie Edson Taylor's sixty-third birthday, people lined up at the foot of Niagara Falls to watch the woman with the far-fetched idea. Excitement crackled in the air.

Upstream on the Niagara River, Annie's big moment arrived. She realized the danger. She also realized this ride would take her farther than over the Falls— it would take her to a future where money would not be a problem.

Annie climbed inside the barrel. Two of her assistants attached the lid, pumped in enough air to last about an hour, and set the barrel drifting.

Annie jostled inside the small, dark barrel, bobbing through the rapids and slamming into rocks. The barrel pitched and rolled forward and back, left and right, and up and down in the rough, tough, bucking-bronco ride.

Pounding sounds of cascading water roared louder and louder as the barrel neared the Falls. Annie gripped her fists to the harness. She snapped her eyes shut and gulped a deep breath. The barrel hurled downward over Niagara Falls.

The crowd stared in wide-eyed wonder as the barrel plunged down, down, down inside a cascade of water. Fifty feet. Tumbling down, down, down. One hundred feet. Tossing, turning down, down, down. One hundred fifty feet. Dropping faster and faster. One hundred sixty-seven feet! The barrel slammed into the pool of misty water beneath the Falls.

All eyes gazed on the mist. Was Annie alive or twisted and broken by the fall? People held their breaths as the barrel bobbed to the surface. A crew waiting at the bottom of the Falls grabbed the barrel with a hook and pulled it to shore seventeen minutes after Annie had climbed inside upriver.

What was the fate of brave Annie Edson Taylor? Did she survive the bone-crushing power of Niagara Falls?

A man unscrewed the top of the barrel and looked inside.

"She's alive!" he called out to the crowd.

Cheers, long and loud, broke loose.

Annie, shaken and bruised with a small cut on her forehead, climbed out of the barrel. She walked among the crowd, still dizzy from the slamming, thrashing, breath-taking ride and said, "Nobody ought ever to do that again."

Annie accomplished her goal and relived her death-defying stunt through the stories she told to crowds of people in her travels. She sold trinkets and posed for photographs with her barrel. One day, her promoter left her, taking her barrel with him. As the money poured in, Annie poured most of it out again trying unsuccessfully to reclaim the barrel.

Fortune escaped Annie, but her dream of fame came true with her biggest idea, barreling over Niagara Falls.

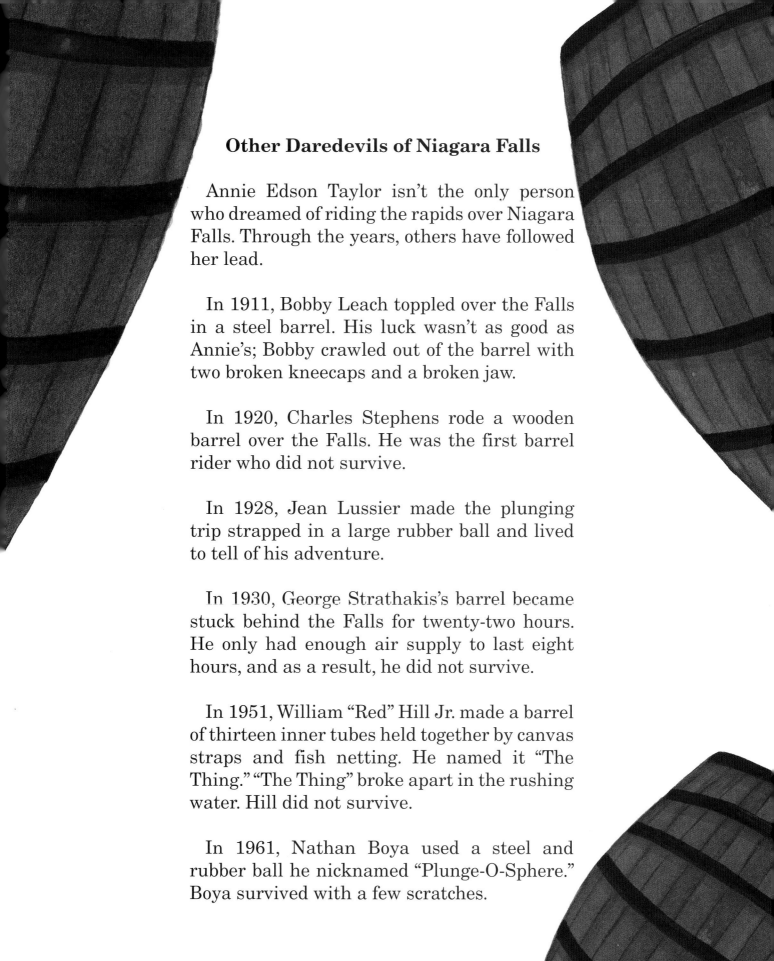

Other Daredevils of Niagara Falls

Annie Edson Taylor isn't the only person who dreamed of riding the rapids over Niagara Falls. Through the years, others have followed her lead.

In 1911, Bobby Leach toppled over the Falls in a steel barrel. His luck wasn't as good as Annie's; Bobby crawled out of the barrel with two broken kneecaps and a broken jaw.

In 1920, Charles Stephens rode a wooden barrel over the Falls. He was the first barrel rider who did not survive.

In 1928, Jean Lussier made the plunging trip strapped in a large rubber ball and lived to tell of his adventure.

In 1930, George Strathakis's barrel became stuck behind the Falls for twenty-two hours. He only had enough air supply to last eight hours, and as a result, he did not survive.

In 1951, William "Red" Hill Jr. made a barrel of thirteen inner tubes held together by canvas straps and fish netting. He named it "The Thing." "The Thing" broke apart in the rushing water. Hill did not survive.

In 1961, Nathan Boya used a steel and rubber ball he nicknamed "Plunge-O-Sphere." Boya survived with a few scratches.

In 1984, Karel Soucek made a barrel of metal and plastic. When his barrel hit the water at the base of the Falls, his arm hit his face. He received a few cuts from his wristwatch.

In 1985, two people took the plunge. In August, Steven Trotter completed his second attempt to drop over the Falls in a barrel wrapped in inner tubes. David Munday rode over in an aluminum and plastic barrel. Munday enjoyed the voyage so much he took the plunge again in 1993, which he survived, but during which he was knocked unconscious.

In 1989, Peter DeBernardi and Jeffrey Petkovich had twice the adventure when they rode together in a barrel over the Falls. Neither was injured.

In 1990, Jessie Sharp attempted to ride over the Falls in a kayak. His body was never found.

In 1995, Steven Trotter made his second trip, but this time Lori Martin was in the barrel with him. Both survived. Three months later, Robert Overacker rode a jet ski over the Falls with the intent to deploy a parachute while in the air. Unfortunately, Overacker's parachute broke away from his body, and he did not survive.

Riding a barrel is not the only way daredevils have conquered Niagara Falls. Tightrope walkers were the first who faced the Falls.

Jean François Gravelet, who named himself the "Great Blondin" because of his blond hair, was the first to walk a tightrope across the deep gorge of the

Niagara River. Beginning in 1859, the Great Blondin made several tightrope walks above the roaring waters. Blondin used a thirty-foot-long pole to keep his balance. On one walk, he carried a man on his back, and on another walk, he pushed a wheelbarrow with a stove in it. He stopped long enough to cook an omelet before finishing the walk. Blondin entertained the audience by standing on his head on the tightrope and making the walk wearing a blindfold. Sometimes on walks, he stretched out on the rope as if taking a nap. Other times, he walked backwards for part of the journey. Once, he walked the rope at night. Spectators followed his walk by watching the lights on the ends of his balancing pole.

In 1860, William Leonard Hunt, the "Great Farini," walked a tightrope across the Niagara River blindfolded and wearing baskets on his feet. Hunt wanted fame as the greatest tightrope walker in the world, so he attempted to outdo the stunts performed by the Great Blondin. On one tightrope walk, Hunt balanced himself on his head. On another, he hung by his toes. He walked the tightrope while carrying a woman. Hunt performed a different stunt with each walk. He fascinated the crowd when he lowered a bucket into the Niagara River and filled it with water. When he pulled up the bucket, he washed a dozen handkerchiefs and then finished the walk.

Maria Spelterini was the first woman to walk a tightrope across the Niagara Falls. She performed her first walk in 1887 and later repeated the stunt blindfolded. Spelterini was a crowd-pleaser, but after performing her last walk with her ankles and wrists bound, she retired from tightrope walking.

Other daredevils have attempted a variety of stunts in the Niagara River and over Niagara Falls. In 2003, Kirk Jones rode the raging river over Niagara Falls wearing only his clothes. He survived with a few bumps and bruises. A number of men and women have braved the Niagara River's whirlpool.

Today, laws ban daredevils from performing stunts at Niagara Falls unless they are given written permission. Some ignore the law. Those who do receive permission to enact their ideas, such as Nik Wallenda in 2012, earn fame and glory as they are watched by hundreds of people.

Are they brave or foolish?